An A – Z Guide on Reinventing Yourself with Compassion and Zeal in the 21st Century

Colleen McInerney

BALBOA.PRESS

A DIVISION OF HAY HOUSE

Balboa Press books may be ordered through booksellers or by contacting:

Balboa Press
A Division of Hay House
1663 Liberty Drive
Bloomington, IN 47403
www.balboapress.com
1 (877) 407-4847

Because of the dynamic nature of the Internet, any web addresses or links contained in this book may have changed since publication and may no longer be valid. The views expressed in this work are solely those of the author and do not necessarily reflect the views of the publisher, and the publisher hereby disclaims any responsibility for them.

The author of this book does not dispense medical advice or prescribe the use of any technique as a form of treatment for physical, emotional, or medical problems without the advice of a physician, either directly or indirectly. The intent of the author is only to offer information of a general nature to help you in your quest for emotional and spiritual well-being. In the event you use any of the information in this book for yourself, which is your constitutional right, the author and the publisher assume no responsibility for your actions.

Any people depicted in stock imagery provided by Getty Images are models, and such images are being used for illustrative purposes only. Certain stock imagery © Getty Images.

Print information available on the last page.

ISBN: 978-1-9822-3694-6 (sc)
ISBN: 978-1-9822-3696-0 (hc)
ISBN: 978-1-9822-3695-3 (e)

Library of Congress Control Number: 2019916216

Balboa Press rev. date: 10/18/2019

I dedicate this book to my husband, Ed, my children Shawn-Wayne and Caitlin-Rae, whose unwavering faith and eternal love are the wind beneath my wings.

ACKNOWLEDGMENTS

I would like thank Shawna Hill for her valuable work in the final setup of this manuscript. Her comments and artistic abilities combined with her skills have helped to make this book what it is. I am eternally grateful to her. She is one of my special angels.

I would also like to thank Ella-Rae Lyall, Nadine Marshall, Mary Amato, Carole Creswell, Cindy Cooke, Linda Aiken, Liberata Infusino and Anne Elizabeth Duff for their faith, encouragement, contributions and unwavering support over the years. They have helped more than they will ever know in the realization of this long held dream of mine.

And lastly, I would like to thank Renka Gesing, for her help in reviewing and partially editing this manuscript. Thank you my special angels.

I preface this A-Z Guide with looking back at pivotal experiences from my youth that helped to form the basis of a system that I have been given and that I have used to guide me in my life. I hope you will find this helpful in guiding you in yours. I have come to believe that there was a universal message given to me on more than one occasion that would benefit everyone. My sincere hope is that this little book can be of assistance to you many times over. It has been designed to include pages that you can return to at any time. Think of your own process as you reread sections and color the alphabetical sheets of your choice.

Life will always hold challenges for you. Just when you conquer one hurdle, you will find others needing to be dealt with, but that is a constant we all must endure. We just need to know that we are not without resources — innate resources that are available to everyone that guide, guard and protect us along the way, regardless of our personal situation.

As a human being you have mental, emotional and spiritual resources available at all times. You needn't have any deep underlying spiritual beliefs in the conventional sense of the word, but if you can acknowledge that *you are Spirit, with a soul, in a body*, then this will not be a stretch of your imagination and will be easy to apply.

The first experience was when I was very young and our family was facing extremely difficult times.

I awoke very early one morning at dusk and got out of bed to go to the bathroom. Standing on either side of the doorway, just inside of my room, were two very tall men dressed from head to toe in gold suits of armor. They wore full-face helmets with an opening near the eyes that looked like a dark void through which I saw no distinguishing features apart from a scintillating, vacuous black energy. They were holding long golden lances that they used to form an X across the open doorway. I immediately understood this to mean that I was not permitted to pass.

Next, I heard one of them say: **"DON'T BE AFRAID."**

The voice was male sounding, full and rich, smooth and kind. Instantly, I found that I was not afraid and they raised their lances to let me pass. I struggle to find adequate words to express how this voice sounded other than to say it sounded like it surrounded me, coming from everywhere at once and wrapping me in a warm velvet cloak. This was to be the first of three times that I would hear this voice in my life. The next times would be some 20 years later in my 20's and again in my 40's.

I passed the guards and walked down a long hallway. At the end of the hall, next to the bathroom was a kitchen. What drew my attention to the kitchen was an unusually bright, white light coming from within. I can still recall standing in the doorway. Peering in I saw a young woman dressed in a long robe, with a veil that partly covered her hair. She was sitting on a straight-backed chair in the center of the room, busily working at a spinning wheel, which I found oddly enough had no yarn attached.

She looked up at me with lovely blue eyes and smiled. Our eyes made contact and she said: **"EVERYTHING IS GOING TO BE ALRIGHT, COLLEEN."**

I didn't speak to her and she didn't say anything else before I turned and went into the bathroom and eventually crawled into the bathtub to wait until others got up. A decision I regretted later in life for not speaking with her or approaching further to ask her why she had chosen to come to me in this way.

When I told my aunt of my experiences, she didn't believe me, saying that I must have been dreaming; but I knew for certain that I had been awake and I did most definitely see and hear what I had relayed. I simply learned not to mention it again.

Soon afterward I found that I had been dropped off at an orphanage to be cared for where I lived for two years. During those days, daycare services were not available and this was a temporary option.

That's where I saw a holy picture in school of the Virgin Mary.

That's the woman in the kitchen, I thought. That's when I realized who the woman in the kitchen actually was. I thought nothing more of the visitation and had forgotten about it until I was back at home with my family a few years later.

In the darkness of my bedroom, after closing my eyes before drifting off to sleep, I would see a shimmering, horizontal, scintillating golden light appear from the horizon of the darkness and as it came forward in my inner vision, it began to shape itself into the visor of one of the guards I had seen. I recognized it immediately and watched in awe until these visions stopped altogether one night. I guess they had achieved the desired effect of reminding me of the visitation and of imprinting the experience in my memory for all time.

I still had my unanswered questions: How did she know my name? Why did she come to me? I had so many questions but I contented myself with at least always remembering her message and whenever I could console someone else with those words, I did. When times were particularly difficult for me, those words had the effect of keeping deep existential fear and desperation at bay. I found peace and contentment in the simplest of things. In the darkest places, I felt guided, guarded and protected with a profound sense of compassion and respect for all sentient beings. Somehow I always knew that everything was going to be alright.

Many years later in my adult life I came to understand that the guards I saw precede and protect Mother Mary and are called warring angels. In my 40's I taught yoga and meditation and one evening a woman came to me afterward saying: **"I don't know if you realize it but the whole time you were teaching I could see a tall man in silver armour standing behind you."** She had the gift of clairvoyance and it was used to validate and confirm what I must have needed to hear at that time.

Oddly enough, over the course of the next years I came to understand that there were people in the right places at the right times all of my life that I can only call my personal angels guiding, guarding and protecting me.

There was a substitute teacher for half of the year in my eighth grade class in Montreal who believed in my potential and could see that I was at risk of becoming a dropout. She was in her early 20's and had not yet finished her teacher's college education. She took a particular interest and chose me as her case study on delinquency in an educational psychology course she was taking at St. Joseph's College in the 1960's.

She came to my home and invited me to her home where she showed me what she was contending with. Her mother had Alzheimer's and was completely unresponsive. She told me that she saw my untapped potential and encouraged me to develop it. She believed in my potential so much that she offered to pay for my college education if I only just finished high-school!

That was a very generous offer but sadly I was unable to finish high school proper and I lost touch with her soon after leaving. I spent 18 months in a group home for girls until I ran away with a friend and we ended up spending six months on the streets of Toronto at the tender age of fifteen. It was a troubling time fraught with life's hurdles yet, somehow, I knew that everything was going to be alright.

I was to experience a wide range of life experiences including homelessness. I saw what life was like for those who are less fortunate. There were people from every walk of life: ordinary men and women who turned to petty crimes for survival, there were hardened criminals with soft hearts and people simply down on their luck, some struggled with addictions and trying to get through another day. There was poverty, loneliness, desperation, isolation, mental illness. People suffered from a variety of problems, but what struck me was that there was an innate goodness. I saw the loyalty, generosity, compassion, kindness and camaraderie that they shared. Somehow I always felt safe with them.

They shared a bond of humanity with one another and with me. And I am grateful to them for their help.

Fortunately for me, six months later, I was able to safely return to my loving family, a stable lifestyle and gainful employment with a bright future ahead; but I never forgot the angels in human form that helped me by taking me under their wing, protecting me from life's imminent dangers. Thank you all.

I tried to reconnect with that kind, young teacher when I had become a new mother in my 30's and returned to finish my education as an adult. I graduated from McGill University with a Bachelor of Education. I wanted to let her know what a profound effect her words and actions had on my life, but I was not successful in finding and thanking her personally. My sincere hope is that I get a chance to thank her one day. Instead, I passed on her gift of support and encouragement to the many students at risk that I had the honour of teaching over subsequent years.

There were friends along the way that were instrumental in setting my feet on the right path to fulfilling my deepest desires. I was aware of their profound influence behind so many of life's unfolding events, twists and turns for which I am eternally grateful to them.

There were others that I met while traveling who literally saved my life.

In my early twenties, I decided to accompany my girlfriend, Josette, on a trip from Canada to Europe and then overland from Turkey to India and Nepal. This was in 1974. We were young and hopeful, innocent and adventurous with no idea of what awaited us on this journey. I had many memorable experiences, two of which were nearly fatal.

The first one found me in Nepal being swept by strong currents down river in the Himalayan mountains. I was unable to get past the midpoint. I was exhausted when suddenly, while floating on my back, I saw in my mind's eye, a two-line obituary printed in black and white in our local newspaper from back home that said:

Colleen McInerney has met her death by drowning in a river of the Himalayan mountains in Nepal...

I then realized the seriousness of my deadly situation. But then I heard a woman's voice calling my name. I fixed my gaze on the cliffs above me and saw the tiny figure of a young woman running towards me, waving frantically and calling my name. This gave me my bearings.

I found the strength to swim a few strokes in her direction and before long my feet were firmly planted on the sandy bottom. I don't recall this woman's name. I just know that she was one of the people who was traveling in Fritz' bus from Europe to Nepal in 1974. I'm eternally grateful to her and hope to get the opportunity to thank her in person one day.

The second experience two months later was much more profound. While having a routine procedure done in a hospital in New Delhi, I found myself leaving my body. I could see my body below me as well as the other people and details in the room, but I was not moved or fretful. I found that I was not emotionally attached to my life or my body and I was barely twenty-four years of age.

Next, came the experience of finding myself in a tunnel that was directly above my head, heading straight up. While contained in the tunnel, I could hear the music of the spheres. I was cognizant of my thoughts and had a quick overview of my life up to that point. I can remember thinking:

Oh, I know what this is. This is the transmigration of my soul.

Oddly enough, I realized that without my body with its many limitations, I was aware of having heightened senses and felt more alive than ever. I was still myself. The mysteries of death were laid bare in that instance. They were right! There is life after death. We are more than the sum of our parts. In fact, we are much, much more.

And then I saw them.

At the end of the dark tunnel, I saw a very bright white light and all around the circle I saw what looked like people standing shoulder to shoulder looking down at me. All I could see were the smokey blue-gray darkened silhouettes of their heads and shoulders as they focused in on me. Then, I saw one man whose face and body was completely illuminated, with one leg and arm outstretched, reaching inward for me to take a hold of his hand and to follow him into the light. I took his hand and went through to the other side. I can remember thinking that this was Jesus and wondering what I had ever done to deserve this distinction.

We walked peacefully side by side, along a wide road without vehicles, where we encountered a few solitary people coming from the opposite direction. We acknowledged them with a nod and entered a long, low-lying building. We walked inside a large room together and stood before a table of people sitting much as a panel of judges might sit. They were facing me while they spoke. I cannot remember what they said but they did speak with me. I can only recall some of my own words and surmise that what they asked me had to do with whom I had loved. My answer was my mother, my friend, Josette and my boyfriend, Don. I later learned the questions asked were: **How have you loved and what have you done with your gifts?**

All I remember next was that I was saddened and disappointed to find that I was no longer standing with Jesus in front of the panel. I seemed to be turned away from them against my will and felt as if I was being swallowed up by the floor beneath my feet. I had not wanted to return to my earthly life but found that I literally had no choice. I was back in my body.

The next morning the anesthetist came to my bedside, put his hand on my heart saying that they thought they "had lost" me last night to which I simply replied: *"You did."*

I understood that I had some things to do in this life that I had not yet accomplished and I would be given the chance to do so. What exactly I was to do remained and still remains a mystery. Has my mission been accomplished on this earth or is this small book in some way part of what I am intended to do? I was given a gift that has helped me, continues to help me and that I know was meant for me to share.

I heard that soft, loving and velvety voice for the second time when I returned from India and was working as a landscape gardener raking leaves when suddenly I became aware of a shift in my consciousness. The land around me became hazy and slightly out of focus. I stopped what I was doing and then I heard the voice coming from behind to envelop me. It said: **"ASK AND YOU SHALL RECEIVE. SEEK AND YOU SHALL FIND. KNOCK AND IT SHALL BE OPEN."**

Unfortunately for me, I did not consciously heed those words until more than ten years later. I was raising two children on my own with very meager financial resources and I realized that everything I had ever deeply desired, I had somehow received and more. Now that I needed to provide a better life for my children, I decided to consciously ask, seek and knock. I had been told years before. But I had let myself believe in scarcity amidst proof to the contrary. It was time to apply what I had been given.

I began to take some time to myself each day, to sit quietly, and in a meditative altered state, I asked for guidance and help going forward in order to provide a good life for myself and my children. We lived in a large, comfortable home that had rent subsidies for people with low income. We always had food, friends and every possible convenience without actually having much money. I was being given what I needed at that time and I was grateful, but I needed to create abundance. I needed well-paying work.

I had tried all of the conventional ways to find a job as a teacher, to no avail. I sought opportunities to be presented to me so I could knock on the appropriate doors at the right time for them to be opened. Sometimes they only opened a crack with part- time teaching, other times they didn't open at all, and I had to understand that they were not in our best interests at that time. I needed to be patient and to keep the faith. I was needed at home in order to be there for my children during the more turbulent times. There had been a brutal murder in my teenaged son's immediate family and one year later his father passed away in an accident. I also had a five-year-old daughter whose father and I were recently separated. Someone needed to be there for them and I was that someone. I needed to remain alert and aware so that I could take advantage of the opportunities as they were presented to me. I also needed to keep the faith as I had no idea what was around the proverbial corner.

By opening up to receive what was in the best interest of all concerned, my priorities were clear, but the way forward was not. Help came from many unexpected people and places over time and our needs were always met.

Seeking to do the right thing, or to know the truth of a situation requires that we listen to our intuition and inspiration and open up to receiving the guidance. I found I received in greater abundance than I would have been capable of creating or imagining on my own. People, places, circumstances perfectly aligned to meet all of our needs. Things eventually did evolve enough for me to notice the paradigm shifts, but at times they were imperceptible and I felt stuck. I just kept the faith that things would be alright. And they most certainly were.

In the early 1980's, when my son was born, I was living in the largest cooperative housing project in Canada, blocks away from Montreal's colleges and universities. I could walk to my classes while I was studying so I was well placed to rent out my extra bedroom to an international student in order to supplement my income. This not only helped me to meet our financial needs, but I made a lifelong friend, another angel on my life's journey.

I struggled for years to find employment in my field of study until one day I made a phone call that changed everything. I had introduced myself, mentioning my qualifications, when the person on the other end said: *"You have been heaven sent!"*

After years of sending off my CV only to be rejected because there was a glut of teachers during those years, I was given a job over the phone without so much as an interview. My task was to educate a troubled teenager who had been permanently expelled at the beginning of an academic school year from an alternative school. I would be teaching her at her home for two hours a day, four days a week. That was an answer to all of our needs. I could understand this young girl, I could be there for my young children when they needed me before and after school and I could be well compensated for the work I was to do. It was the perfect job for the time that then transitioned me on to other opportunities. I never looked back. The time had come and I was ready, willing and able to do my part.

At that time, the car that I relied on to get me to work and back in time to meet the school bus for my five-year old daughter needed expensive repairs and every time I got behind the wheel of my car I asked Spirit to get me to my destination safely in time to return and receive my children at the end of the day. Fortunately for everyone I was always home on time, but my car was getting slower and slower on takeoff. The clutch was going to go at any time and I had a lot of highway driving to do before payday.

One night I was awakened by three very odd sounds simultaneously: a high pitched whine (**EEEEE**), a distinctive white noise (**SHHHHH**), and a garbled sound much like tuning into radio frequencies.

That's when I was made to understand, *It's just Spirit, go to sleep*, but I hadn't forgotten.

A few days later, I was awakened again, only this time there were only the first two sounds simultaneously: the high pitched whine and the white noise. The energy frequencies had been adjusted and that's when I heard the velvety voice for the third time.

"I AM GOING TO HELP YOU GET ANOTHER CAR."

Within a little more than a week, I received a phone call from my old friend Josette, who lived over an hour away in the countryside where her brother owned a car dealership. What she said next was music to my ears. *"Colleen, my brother wants me to change my car, but it's still good and I can't think of anyone else I would rather give it to than you."*

You can't imagine how heaven-sent that sounded to me at the time. I agreed to pick it up on the upcoming Sunday. Miraculously, my car died at the student's home on the Friday! I was driven to Alain's home where we signed the papers sitting at his kitchen table on a sunny Sunday afternoon. I never skipped a beat returning to work on the following Monday morning with another car.

Two years later Josette called saying that her brother had a car on his lot that might interest me. I drove for over an hour on the highway, stopped the car at the front door to the office on the lot and went inside. I decided to take the car and was asked to park my car on the side, which I tried to do, but when I got into the car I found it would not start. It never started again. Coincidence? I doubt it.

So, as you can see here, Spirit works in strange ways. Ways we never would have been able to plan or execute on our own. They elicit help from people on our life's path to help us like the young substitute teacher who believed in me and helped me to believe in myself; like the lady on the cliff's edge who literally saved me from drowning; or the school administrator who handed me the perfect job over the phone where my gifts and abilities would be put to good use for the highest good of all concerned; as well as my good friend and her brother providing the car I so desperately needed, just to mention a few interventions by my human angels. There were too many of these interventions to mention here. Timing was everything. Perfect in every way. Better than I would ever have hoped for, to the point of being one step ahead of my conscious awareness. I have not heard the voice of Spirit so clearly or concisely since. At least not directly. But I am well aware of the influences in my life over the years. My children and I have continued to be guided, guarded and protected. I see mini-miracles all the time occurring in people's lives.

Even if it seemed to take a very long time in coming, doors opened at the appropriate time as a direct result of consciously asking, seeking and knocking. The people I met on the path, the relationships that would develop, the opportunities that presented themselves were all pieces of the puzzle of our mutual personal growth and evolution.

All it took from me was to get control of my emotionalized thoughts and through honest, sincere, connected introspection, decide what I needed at that time in my life.

I needed to put it in the positive, to ask, seek and knock, remain aware and open minded, use discernment, remain committed to the highest good of all concerned, including my own. I had to commit to sincerely doing my part by opening up to receive in the positive and to trusting in my own unique process.

However slowly I thought change took place, in retrospect, it was constantly moving forward, bit by bit, thought by thought, moment by moment, lesson by lesson, sign post by sign post, person by person. I was just too close to see it objectively or too impatient for the appropriate time and circumstances to present themselves. I didn't give up, however, and by remembering and implementing the wise, loving words of counsel and guidance that I had received and by using the tools I had picked up along the way to connect body, soul and spirit, I found myself receiving in untold, innumerable ways. And you will too. In retrospect, I had no money to speak of, but I was always happy, grateful, and surrounded by abundance that came to me in many different ways. I just hadn't realized its full significance in my life. The scarcity principle is a noxious self-perpetuating weed that needs pruning. I realized I needed help in getting out of this mindset and was successful by working in the positive over time.

My personal experiences and private life were one thing I was able to connect up the dots for, but after dealing with extenuating circumstances and situations that life had in store for my extended family, I saw on another level how Spirit works. Out of something absolutely devastating and painful like the loss of a life tragically taken in a person's prime. Eventually some good did come. This lead to the changing of the laws here in Canada for anyone suspected of rape or murder now being obliged by law to consent to a DNA test, with those results admissible in a court of law. Somehow, good did come out of the violence, chaos and pain leaving important, positive change in its wake.

We cannot always connect up all the dots in life and put a nice pretty bow on the horrors that exist in this world. This is not the message here. The message here is simple. Just know that you are much more than the sum of your parts and as you think so shall you be. You can only control your thoughts around situations in order to learn and grow. Work with whatever you have been given for the highest good. Elicit the help you will need to help you make the changes you would like to see in your life. In the moment things may not make any sense, but stay strong and keep the faith as the results will be made clear over time.

To quote Richard R. Johnson from his book, Lessons In Life, Messages from the Masters, no longer in print or circulation:

$$\text{God} = \text{Individuality} \times \text{Free Will}$$
$$= \text{Desire} + \text{Attitude} (+ -)$$
$$= \text{Miracle} (+ -)$$
$$= \frac{\text{Time}}{\text{Faith}}$$

$$\frac{\text{Miracles} (+ -)}{} $$
$$= \text{Desire} + \text{Attitude} (+ -)$$
$$= \frac{\text{Time}}{\text{Faith}}$$

So, there you have it. A simple equation, I agree, but the message is profound. You are an individual with free will.

What you choose to create in this life will manifest as a direct result of the desires and attitudes that you held in place with your beliefs and thoughts over time and made decisions from there. Knowing this, you can make conscious decisions to review and to change those outdated attitudes and beliefs that are no longer useful or helpful in your life. Knowing this empowers you as never before to create your happiness and contentment in life. You must, however, not forget that you have more than just your limited physical mind, body and hands with which to work when working at this more soulful level.

You are Spirit: unconditional light, love and truth. When you need help in your life, tap into this wellspring by going within and connecting the conscious, subconscious, and super-subconscious levels of yourself. This is where you begin to sow those creative seeds of change and set that blueprint in motion.

We all have weaknesses, limits and issues that we face in our ego personalities, but there are powerful unseen hands at our disposal that need only to be acknowledged, trusted and then to be given the permission to work with, and for, our highest good. And suddenly our life's goals, desires, and ambitions are being given priority, activated, brought to the fore, to be created over time in some unique way. We just need to do our part as it is presented to us and move forward.

You will be required to be honest with yourself, to learn from and act on valuable lessons as you go. Don't be afraid to listen to that wise, compassionate and loving inner voice and to let life evolve in its own perfect time when working in the positive.

Be patient when you are asking, seeking and knocking and above all, keep the faith as you move forward and evolve for your highest good and the highest good of all concerned.

You are expanding your consciousness to include a fuller idea of Self to help you on your journey of life. A loving, non-judgmental, self-affirming resource is always at your disposal; desiring only the highest good of all concerned for you and not necessarily only accessible, or belonging to, any specific sect or religion, but to all of mankind.

The word "God" in the equation above was a direct quote, a word most people would recognize as expressing the Divine, Creative Life-force, Universe, Allah, Mohammed, Krishna, Buddha, Jesus or any name given to a higher power of your belief system. The divine creative life force, however, is a universal life-force regardless of the name you use or your religious beliefs. It does not discriminate.

"For what it's worth: it's never too late or, in my case, too early to be whoever you want to be. There's no time limit, stop whenever you want. You can change or stay the same, there are no rules to this thing. We can make the best or the worst of it. I hope you make the best of it. And I hope you see things that startle you. I hope you feel things you never felt before. I hope you meet people with a different point of view. I hope you live a life you're proud of. If you find that you're not, I hope you have the courage to start all over again."

– Eric Roth

Agency, Ask, Attract

To attract what you want to bring into your life, begin with a positive attitude. Take stock of what you do have, then get in touch with your personal desires, your passion, or whatever brings joy and awe, peace or wonder into your life.

Instead of going "out there" in search of what you want to bring into your life, you will be "going within" and attracting it to you, sowing the seeds of change. You need to know that you have agency over your life. Only you can set the course for implementing the changes you want to see in your life.

Meditation, oracle, prayer, intention, creative visualizations are some of the many ways that you can invoke the assistance to draw what you need to yourself, to clear the path leading you to manifesting your heart's desires. Choose whatever approach appeals to you, depending on your belief system.

Simply go within and sincerely visualize or ask for help with divine intervention in the form of inspiration, guidance and opportunities going forward from here to be presented to you in the areas of concern. Ask in the form of an emotionalized command, not as a wish or a favour. We all know that wishes don't come true. There's no need to bargain as that doesn't work either. Show your appreciation by adding: **"that or better. Thank you in advance."** This takes asking and seeding to another level by adding gratitude and faith into the equation. They are what will set the positive wheels of change in motion. Then let go and keep the faith. Be aware. Pay attention to what comes to you over time.

To bring abundant awe, peace and joy into your life you will tap into what makes you happy. You will need to be honest with yourself here and look at what your personal gifts and abilities are. These are your strengths. You may not know what the full extent of those gifts and abilities are, but if you keep a running record of what you enjoy doing or are interested in learning more about, you will be on the right track. Often we are too humble or unaware of what those gifts could be and they never get developed.

You may have the gift of insight, compassion, communication, rhythm, athleticism, empathy, voice, a love of nature, children, gardening, designing, repairing, building, cooking, creating or appreciating art or music, just to name a few. Find the time to include some in your daily life. You don't need to compete, to excel, or to be the best in order to find means of including them in your life and in expressing them. The object is not to become famous, but to allow ourselves to become the very ones we came here to be.

Don't be afraid; everything is going to be alright.

2

Beliefs

Faithfully sowing and then tending to the seeds of change and leaving them to grow in their own time without questioning the process before you is a necessary step that requires you to have faith that you will reap what you have sown. It's a law. Changes will come in their own time. Here is where you need to believe that you will eventually reap what you have sown.

It may surprise you when you become aware of the bounty you will receive, better than you could have imagined.

By putting forward your request and adding **"that or better"** you will receive what is in your best interests at that time and continue moving forward from there. It's a step-by-step process.

To prove the point, you just need to look at who you have become so far. There were many elements at work over time; societal norms, family values and positive or limited negative belief systems and particular events beyond your control would most likely have been at the core of how you thought yourself to be and thus became.

If you want to change yourself in any way you really need to look at the beliefs you held that brought you here and debunk them as necessary to bring about positive change.

Balance

There is a balance to maintain in all areas of your life, but there is also a balance to maintain between your positive and negative beliefs. Think of any negative or limiting elements in your life as weeds in your garden that require attending to with courage, dignity and perseverance. Eventually the issues get resolved leaving more room for your garden of life to flourish.

Blueprint

By opening up to receive guidance, inspiration, opportunities and help going forward, you will have elicited the help you need in creating an **etheric blueprint** that can be fleshed out for you over time.

Build a strong foundation of change by including your gifts and abilities as joyful seeds to assist you in planting your soulful inner garden. Your life is your personal garden. You are the only one who can decide what to do with it. Fortunately, you have assistants at the ready. Since you have free will, they are waiting for you to ask for their help in order to assist you in unique and untold ways.

Breath

Become aware of the gift of breath you have been freely given. Every part of your body relies on it. Check in on your breath occasionally. Is it too shallow? Are you breathing too quickly? Do you hold your breath when you are concentrating on a task, for example? Pay attention to how you are breathing and feeling. Are you feeling calm? If not, you can use conscious breathing to return to a state where you feel calm, composed, level-headed and grounded in the moment.

Focus in on your breath and your feelings. Before inhaling fully, begin with a slow and full exhale of all the air in your lungs. As you exhale, let go of the tension you feel in your body. Now, mark how this feels.

Then, inhale slowly and completely. Continue taking full, deep, relaxing breaths, releasing all tensions on the exhale, and mark how this feels. This can become your new point of reference, to refer back to in times when you realize that you are out of balance. A few, long, full, deep breaths will help you to return to a more relaxed state.

Conflicts and creative change

When your underlying belief systems are not congruent with the changes you want to see in your life, conflicts arise.

Pay attention to the beliefs you have like: **"I want to but..."** fill in the blanks. This push/pull dichotomy causes a stalling effect. **"I want to and..."** is more freeing and will begin the process of moving forward.

We need to step outside of our everyday reality for a few minutes each day to tend to our seedlings of change by remembering that cohesive thought and action will bring about whatever we have set in motion. Understand that you are in the process of change in its myriad of forms and just believe in yourself.

As certain as you have a body needing nourishing, attention and grooming, you also have an inner garden where your inner Self resides. Connect to it when tending to, pruning and grooming your everyday life. If you don't actively connect with it, life will take over and plant its seeds chaotically and you will be reacting to life rather than actively creating it.

You want to create a better, more fulfilling life for yourself. A repetitive cycle of planting seeds and then pulling up the seedlings soon afterward will never give you the garden that you desire. You need to nurture those seedlings, weed around them and let them grow in their own time before you can benefit from their yield.

What creative change looks like for you is limitless in the total scheme of things. It's up to you to use your own desires, beliefs, tools, skills, creativity with tenacity of purpose to assist in creating it over time. The key here is to use your tools in the positive and not to cynically or negatively throw up your hands and give in to the status quo.

Conflicting times of doubt

It seems that along the way when we venture out with faith and determination something happens to put doubt into the mix. Keep negative doubt at bay. Those conflicting times of doubt are perfect saboteurs. They succeed in stopping our progress out of fear, self-doubt, apathy, lethargy, procrastination. Use your creative imagination to envision a positive solution. Whatever you can imagine, you can create.

Cornucopia

Imagine a full cornucopia positioned just within reach above your head that has your name on it, but you will be required to reach out and to claim your harvest. You might even have to wait or to work for it. Yours is a unique life. Time and process lie in the eternal present moment and will show you the way forward.

Denial

You may be asking yourself whether this positive thinking, asking, seeding and believing positive change will come is just another form of denial.

Denial is difficult to ascertain at first. When we don't believe that we will eventually succeed, due to previously failed attempts, we have placed a cog in the proverbial wheel. We prove ourselves to be correct and won't succeed.

Denial is an outright lie to oneself. We know when we are lying to ourselves.

It would be more correct to say that we are in denial when we believe that we cannot bring about positive change into our lives. We will most definitely have denied ourselves the opportunities and thus shut the door to positive change.

Desires

We are never in denial by stating our heartfelt desires as simple truths, aims and goals. Desires need to be authentic coming from within. We know that we are not in denial by expressing them.

The problem may be that we stopped even desiring change believing it to be impossible. This is a limiting and negative belief that needs revamping. Change takes many forms, as unique as there are people on the planet and is a constant whether we know it or not. As long as you draw breath, positive change is possible.

Inner Dialogues

Your inner dialogues needn't be such a stretch for you. How you phrase your desires matters here. Keep them in the positive, keep them attainable by refraining from stalling with negativity and know that you are in the developmental phase of your life. This will take some time to come to fruition.

Discernment

Discernment is needed here. Don't just aim to win the lottery. However long change may take, or whatever form it eventually does take, remains to be seen. Put yourself in the driver's seat and hold on because things are going to start to change. You will get there.

Emancipation

Emancipation is what you are after. The past remains in the past. You are going to use your energy to your advantage and move forward taking with you the valuable lessons learned from life's past experiences, but the key here is you are moving forward.

Excuses

Abandon the excuses as they will no longer serve you, i.e.: **"I know, but in my case..."** fill in the blanks.

None of that matters any longer. When change is what you are after excuses are only more stall tactics. Find a work-around, otherwise you continue to mark time, slowing progress. Eradicate the excuses any way that you can by shedding rational light on them. They are completely irrational. They are the weeds or stumbling blocks put in your path by your own limiting belief system. There is always a way around them by becoming aware of what they are, where they came from and then thanking them and letting them go, as they can no longer serve you in moving towards what you want to experience. Supplant them with your well-chosen seeds of change instead and nurture those.

Evolution

You are always evolving, whether positively or negatively. You are always moving as nothing stays the same in this world. Not a cloud or blade of grass. Why would you be any different?

Embrace what comes for you to work with. We have all heard the expression you are what you eat. Well, the same applies here: you are what you embrace, what you espouse, what you endeavor to do. You may not see your evolution taking place, as the increments may be small, but over time they are obvious to all who have eyes to see.

Encouragement

Encourage yourself by being empowered in the moment. If you veer off course simply take a deep breath and return to the present moment with renewed optimism.

Fear

Fear has its place in our lives. If we are in imminent danger or if we know or suspect that something is just wrong, then fear is useful to remind us to get out of the way or not to enter into a compromising situation. This is rational fear. It will act as a guide to help steer us in the right direction.

Where we are misguided is when fear is the dominant emotion in our lives. Irrational fear, doubt, panic, and anxiety does not steer us in the right direction. We freeze, get stuck and feel disempowered. Fear may be causing us to under react or overcompensate with excessive, compulsive or dangerous behaviour. Chronic irrational fear can manifest as mental, emotional and physical rigidity holding us back from realizing our potential, causing tension, unrealistic limitations and disease.

Irrational fear and doubt may not be completely understood because there are many ramifications and guises for fear. We may not always recognize them for what they are and they can sabotage our efforts. We may not even realize that we are afraid because we have tuned out and turned off the messages. That's how powerful and painful fear can be. But we remain stuck there.

Holding patterns chronically held like unconsciously twisting, flexing, holding or clenching hands, feet, teeth, jaws, breath or any other internal muscles in the body have their beginnings in fear.

We don't need to remember why these chronic holding patterns are there, but we can work on becoming aware of what they are. After a while pain and inflammation

23

will let you know they are there. Check your posture, the alignment of your head, neck, shoulders, jaw and all of the muscles down to your toes. Check in and consciously relax that area as you exhale.

Actively let go of that tension by focusing on your breath for a moment and then slowly and thoroughly exhale through your slightly pursed lips. Consciously drop down into your body, notice the areas of tension and let them go. You will feel an immediate release where tension is chronically being held. Every now and then check into what holding patterns you have and keep consciously realigning and releasing it until you realize one day that you no longer need to.

Fear is the opposite of love. It will only hold you back where love will set you free. Flip that fear into its opposite, love, any way that you can. It begins with your thoughts.

What are you thinking? Are your fears helping or hindering your progress? your health? your happiness? There are some common fears like the fear of abandonment, of the unknown, of ridicule, shame, exposure, rejection; or hidden fears may be left over from past traumas, previous failures or even of the fear of success itself. Replace any residual fears or fear-based thoughts with loving, kind words of advice and encouragement to help you on your way.

When dealing with deeply-rooted fears, thinking thoughts of love and positivity are like shedding a light into the darkness, illuminating the way forward. This will help you to go forward with confidence in finding a creative solution. Everything will be alright.

Fear is the most prolific weed in our garden of life that needs lots of pruning to eventually eradicate, or at best, to keep under control. Actively working on letting go of fear and its effects on our lives and our bodies is required maintenance in our garden of life. Fear is the cog in the wheel of love and positivity. It keeps cropping up here and there in our lives, derailing our attempts. It needs more attention as it is a noxious weed.

Moving forward past the fear

You may find yourself going forward and then falling back out of habit, but remember to catch yourself, forgive and forget and continue to shed rational light on the issues in order to continue going forward in the moment. Unconditionally. Aiming to go forward is the opposite of looking backward. It flows naturally and feels fabulous. If you aren't sure, ask yourself: **"How does this feel?"** If you are feeling positive and empowered then you know you are on the right track.

Guilt

We have all done and said things in our past that we are ashamed of, but, if we have learned from them, then we are free to forgive and to let them go. Flagellation serves no purpose. It's another negative stall tactic that only gets in the way of progress. If you find that you are beating yourself up, gently stop yourself by closing your eyes and using kind words of encouragement to stop those thoughts in their tracks. You can only think one thought at a time. Make it constructive.

Offer yourself unconditional forgiveness. Guilt actually gets in the way of feeling worthy. If you replace the shame-based thoughts with kinder words of forgiveness you will have changed the course of your thoughts. Forgive yourself and let it go by being in the moment and using the time constructively to build yourself up.

Gifts

Acknowledge that you deserve to be happy in this life and that you have unique gifts to discover, develop and to share. They are your birthright. They are your personal and unique contribution. Give them room to develop and grow.

You may not be aware of what your gifts are. There may be some that you recognize and some that are recognized by other people. They may see you in a role you never considered for yourself.

You may have many gifts waiting to be discovered. Don't be too humble or too brash, but allow yourself to explore the numerous possibilities available to you. Try different things that make you happy. Make them an integral part of your daily life.

Prioritize your time to include personal development. Read up on what interests you, take courses, watch and learn from others. Try your hand at whatever it is that calls to you. You will be glad that you did.

Gratitude

Whenever possible express your gratitude inwardly for all that is good in your life and for what you have, see, feel and know. The more that you are grateful, the more you will have to be grateful for; because like attracts like, gratitude begets more to be grateful for.

When you are open to receiving in the positive, it is imperative that your mindset is in alignment with what it is that you are to draw to yourself and not remain focused on what you do not yet have. This push/pull dichotomy is getting in the way of moving forward and keeps you stuck.

Goals

Set clear and realistic goals for yourself in all good conscience, then call forth, visualize, or ask for the help you will need to attain these, ending with **"that or better for the highest good of all concerned. Thank you in advance."** Let go and go with the flow, keeping a discerning open mind. Learn and grow.

Happiness

Develop and hone the gifts and abilities that come to you honestly. They will bring pure joy, direction and purpose into your life. What if you could live in this state? More to the point, why can't you?

Don't hold back the powerful urges for creativity and change when they arise in your life. Your physical, mental, emotional, financial and even spiritual health is dependent on having a positive flow of energy. Don't hold it back.

Hope

Hope cannot be understated. The end results are not what matters here. Hope will carry you through the more difficult times and in the end, the results will eventually be revealed. If you lose hope, sit quietly and have that supportive talk with yourself. Refrain from those negative voices in your head that will have you giving up before you even have a chance of success. If what you want is not in your best interests, you must remain realistic and adapt accordingly.

Habits

If you struggle with old habits, instead of trying to do battle with them, just make new ones. When they become habitual you will notice that you have outgrown the undesirable ones. For the more challenging and difficult problems you are facing habitually, you will need some help to get where it is you want to be in your life. You can achieve this by something I call, **I watching me.**

I watching me

"I" refers to the super-subconscious or spiritual Self. The High Self — the Spirit that is in the form of you. Some would call this their Divine Self. This is the wise, generous and loving Self, the one who hears your thoughts and prayers and is always ready to give you the help you need. But you must ask in the form of a command, give permission to receive that help and trust in the process over time.

"I" can be seen as reaching a hand out for you to grasp in order to move forward safely.

You can connect or attune to this part of yourself by quietly going deep within. It doesn't matter if you don't have the ideal circumstances. You can be on a bus, train, plane or be taking a walk for instance. If possible, just close your eyes, focus in on your breath, let go of the tension in your body, relax and go within, thus connecting the conscious mind with the subconscious mind, then put your request for assistance in a particular matter forward in good faith. And leave it there, ending with: "**that or better. Thank you in advance**".

The sub-conscious can be equated with the soul self and is the medium that you use to connect to your super-subconscious, Spirit or High Self. It acts as a bridge or a conduit carrying your messages across. It can be seen as The Messenger.

From this perspective, "I" can look down upon the "me" who struggles from time to time with life's hurdles or challenges, offering pure unconditional love, compassion, understanding wisdom, patience, protection and help

to clear the path of obstacles put in your way. It can put people, places, opportunities, assistance and guidance on your path, which if heeded can be used as the instruments you need to move ahead.

"I" can help "me" in unfathomable, unique ways. Always. Don't worry if you aren't sure of being successful in achieving this state of union. It's natural. You just aren't aware of the subtle shifts in consciousness yet. It's who you are!

Relying solely on the conscious, or ego self-called "me", is not enough to get through the most difficult, doubtful times. So, just go within to access your personal, higher power. This is where you turn for help and guidance with your desires, problems or needs. This is where your gardener and unseen workers reside, where the work takes place that brings fruition.

Champion yourself in this way by connecting, communing and trusting in the wisdom and love that is always available to you. It will never steer you wrong. This is your personal power. It's there for you regardless of your life circumstances.

From this perspective, when there are words that you need to hear, that you may always have longed to hear, say them to yourself with tenderness. You will get the courage, guidance, assistance and strength you need.

Once you have consciously connected yourself to this personal power, state your needs or desires clearly and allow the time necessary for things to unfold. Sometimes we have a tendency to give up because we have put negativity into the mix, thus canceling the process that we had started in good faith. Sometimes the things that are being presented seem counter intuitive. Perhaps you are being given the clear message to work on other areas of yourself first.

Power of Intention

Take some quiet, contemplative time with a pen and paper and write out columns:

I think... I feel... I want... I need... and fill in the blanks here. State them in the positive. For example, if you want a particular result, how you word it matters here. Your subconscious does not recognize the words "not" or "no". You can always adapt or adjust as you go; but put things down on paper first in the positive form. This will focus your requests, needs and desires to be able to attract them to you in this lifetime. You can keep this list in plain sight to remind you of what they are.

Clear and honest communication is easily understood and no one can fault you for your thoughts, feelings, wants and needs — not even yourself. Begin here. Use the power of intention to set your sights. Then go within and work towards attracting them into your life, ending with: "**that or better for the highest good of all concerned. Thank you in advance**."

Judge and Jury

There will be some junk you will need to eliminate in your life: attitudinal, physical, mental, emotional, relational or spiritual "stuff" that needs to be reassessed, revised and let go of. This requires reaching for the help available from a soulful rather than a mental level. This requires you to take a break for a few minutes in a day from working things out continuously in your conscious mind, thus getting out of your head and appealing to your heart and soul for the assistance you need. Then you must listen to, or in some way recognize, the wisest counsel that eventually finds its way to you and heed that.

One such thing needing to be dealt with is your inner judge and jury, your saboteur. This is the part of you that believes you are not good enough or smart enough: compares, doubts, puts your down, blames, scolds, procrastinates, agonizes, catastrophizes, chastises, criticizes, limits you or scoffs at your attempts. Shed some rational light on these saboteurs by playing around with them for a bit. Blow them all out of proportion. Take them to the limit and laugh at their absurdity. They are all stultifying negative voices that have the effect of triggering you or shutting you down, blocking your progress. See them for what they are.

Whenever you are aware of harsh, self-pitying, cruel or judgmental thoughts and want to stop them in their tracks, say: **"Cancel, cancel"** and deliberately take control by replacing this negativity with positive advice and supportive loving words, thus silencing the critical judge and jury.

Talk to yourself whenever you are aware of your critical inner voice creeping in and replace it with:

"Cancel. Cancel. That's OK, you are just doing that again. You can let it go now. Everything is going to be alright."

Do this as many times as you need to, for as long as it takes to break the pattern. Canceling this voice will give you back the hope and the joy you so desire and deserve and let you get on with the real job at hand — personal growth, self-emancipation and positive change.

Journey

On the particular journey that you have embarked upon there is no room for stultifying, limiting voices in your own head that only serve to hold you back from getting closer to your joy in life.

Joy

We all experience a full range of emotions in a day, but joy should also be one of them. Hopefully it's a preponderant one. If it isn't, begin there. Ask. Seek. Knock.

Inner Knower

You have an inner wisdom, an inner-knower. Some people refer to this as their common sense, their sixth sense, their felt sense, their guidance, their intuition, their High Self. We need to pay attention to this part of ourselves because inevitably we err when we ignore it. How many times have you had some regrets and heard yourself in retrospect saying: "I knew it!" Yes, you did know it, but you ignored it, or you rationalized it away before checking on your presuppositions or niggling thoughts on the matter.

You need to listen to that inner voice that speaks to you, only and especially if it sounds true and wise. Differentiate between the fear-based, negative, societal inner voices dancing around in your head and the wise, loving ones with good solid counsel and clear impressions and heed those inner voices because they have your best interest at heart.

Kindness

We often treat others with kindness, so we know what it is to be kind. We need to practice being patient and kind with ourselves. This is not selfish, it is self-affirming. We need to be kind and patient with ourselves at all times, but particularly in times of change in order to stay the course without giving up at the first signs of conflict. We need to be honest and truthful with ourselves. Being honest with yourself doesn't mean you have to be brutal. Honesty with kindness is the balance you need to strike.

If you are aware of areas of your personality that are keeping you stuck in a rut, then be honest with yourself. Ask yourself what it is that needs to change and make this an area that you will work on. You won't change everything overnight, but with kind, loving counsel and patience as well as perseverance, you will succeed.

If you are in a relationship or a job that is destructive, it is unhealthy for you. If you need to work on plucking up the courage and strength to move on, go within and ask for help in this area of your life and do your part by acting on the information and opportunities that will be presented to you over time. If you still aren't sure of what it is that you should do, then perhaps it would be helpful to imagine that same situation in the life of someone you love, say a child or best friend, and think of what it is that you would advise this person to do for themselves. This might help give you more clarity and a way forward.

Knock

When you have gone within and asked, by sowing seeds of change, you have created this blueprint that will go out into the ethers to seek out what you need to help bring about changes and opportunities. All you need to do for your part is to knock on the metaphoric doors as they are presented to you.

Some of these doors will remain closed; just know they were not in your best interest. Some will lead you to work on yourself in order to get to the next level of development to receive in the positive, while other doors will open up wide, presenting you with opportunities to learn and to grow, to move in the direction of your heart's desires.

Pay attention. Be aware and watch for the synchronicities. Listen to that wise, kind, inner-knower and go forward with confidence.

Love

We need to give ourselves the love, forgiveness and the fresh start that we seek. When we are in need of reassurance, guidance, help with a difficult issue, that's when we need to champion ourselves.

Look into a mirror. Look into your eyes with the purest of intentions and complete sincerity. Have a talk with yourself.

Do this from a place of love and respect, for the one looking back at you is yourself.

Tell yourself what you know to be true. This is healing. This is grounding. It validates and reconnects us. Tell yourself, with all sincerity what you have longed to hear. Search your heart and soul. Don't wait for it to come from outside of yourself. It may never come and if it does it often has conditions attached.

This honest talk with ourselves is not frivolous. It makes us feel heard, loved, connected, safer, more secure. It strips away some of the walls, or blockages, that were created to protect us from feeling the vulnerabilities and pain we experienced in life, but those blockages also kept our true untapped feelings and potential out of our grasp and kept us stuck, numb, tuned out.

Ask yourself: **How can I love myself more?** And pay attention to the answers. Write them down. If you start working from here, to aim for your highest good, you will have a good starting point. Ask for help in very specific areas that you have synthesized down to the causes to the issue at hand,

and work to change those stumbling blocks. You will know what they are.

Then, go within, to visualize, seed, or to ask for what you want or need. End with saying, **"that or better for the highest good of all concerned. Thank you in advance"** and leave it, knowing you have set a course in motion. Pay attention to whatever comes your way and do your part.

Lessons

As long as you live you never stop learning. You have the choice to choose between learning through love or learning through fear. Lessons will come in many forms, usually presented to us during the most difficult times of our lives. When this is the case, ask yourself: "What can I learn from this? Is there a recurring pattern here?

Learning

A mantra that you can repeat as a simple affirmation of intent to help you is: **I choose to learn through love and joy.**

This sets the direction of where you want to head. Situations and opportunities will be presented to help you to navigate, learn and develop through love and joy and not through confrontation and fear. There will always be lessons pointing you in the more loving directions that are up to you to discern.

A big lesson to learn is to set clear limits and boundaries with yourself and others. We will know if this is the case because we will have had many lessons or difficult tests along the way in order to teach us this or any other valuable lessons.

There is learning and there is acting upon or applying what you have learned. Once the lessons have become a part of who you are, you will find that personal growth has taken place and these particular tests have stopped. Suddenly you will have moved on to other lessons.

Meditation or Meditative prayer

It is from here that you can do your most valuable work of asking, seeking, knocking and seeding for the highest good of all concerned.

Meditation or meditative prayer does not mean repeating Sanskrit words or strict adherence to religious dogmas or practices. There are no uncomfortable positions and principles that may hold no meaning for you or that go against your particular religious beliefs. This is the time where you seem to be doing little or nothing at all but it is the time you take for yourself to get in touch with your deep inner Self. It is the most important time of your day where you set aside the minutia of life and feel more alive and free. Personalize yours.

When you meditate, you are stilling the conscious every-day rational mind, sometimes known as The Trickster, that can steer you hither and yon on some logic or other that suits your fancy — and that, can be a very fickle and irrational way to govern your life. Getting out of the ego mind and dropping down to the level of the sub-conscious, or soul mind, your visualizations or heartfelt requests will be carried forward by The Messenger, your sub- conscious mind, to be fleshed out much like a blueprint that will come to fruition over time.

Simply sit in a comfortable position that supports your body well. Sometimes when we go deeply within, our head may roll forward or we may feel like we are falling to one side and this can become distracting and uncomfortable.

Once you are well supported, focus on your breath as you inhale slowly through your nose and exhale slowly and completely through your slightly pursed lips. Breathe in love, and exhale love, for the highest good of all concerned. If your mind wanders, return to focusing on your breath. After a few deep breaths, you will feel calm, relaxed and centered.

When you are feeling calm, centered and relaxed, scan your body for any chronically held tensions and let them go on the exhale. The exhale facilitates a greater release. You will feel like you are dropping into a state of peace and from there you will sow your seeds of change.

This is when you begin sowing those seeds of change you want to attract to your life. Whenever your mind wanders too far from your original intentions before you are finished, return to your conscious breathing as this will help you to refocus your mind and return to the creative demand.

At some point you may feel as if you have fallen asleep, but don't worry, the sub-conscious does not sleep and your intentions and requests will still have been brought forward to your Higher Self to be fleshed out. You have simply gone deeply within to another level of consciousness.

It is in this peaceful place that you will find your true source of power. There is no judge or jury standing guard, no critical, negative voice exists to disrupt your peace. You are a pure being and as such you are at your most peaceful, powerful and creative to effectively sow the seeds of change that you desire to bring into your life.

When your requests are more general and non-specific, for example, if you want to realize your potential in this lifetime, or to find the perfect job, partner in life, etc., or you need help and guidance in a particular area of your life or personality but you do not know where to start, call forth the assistance, the clarification and the opportunities that you need help with by simply stating:

USE ME IN MY CAPACITY FOR THE HIGHEST GOOD OF ALL CONCERNED. THANK YOU IN ADVANCE.

If you have a particularly specific and clear idea of what it is that you want, make your emotionalized command and finish with:

...that or better, for the highest good of all concerned. Thank you in advance.

Natural Law

Mother Nature holds the key to the simple natural laws and rhythms in life. Find a natural environment and spend time connecting there. Relax. Listen. Watch. Feel. Explore. Think. Wonder. Enjoy.

Think about the perfection that you see all around you. Notice how effortlessly everything flows. The trees, water, plants and lands do not put up any resistance to natural laws. They go with the flow, grow, bend and flex in order to survive. Flowers, plants and trees don't just try to grow. They grow. Water flows around or over obstacles put in its path. It's natural law.

Everything co-exists peacefully. Every need is met. Birds, bees, flowers, trees, plants, animals, fish and invertebrates are all functioning in perfect harmony to get their needs met and they keep the natural balance in place.

We are not immune to natural laws. There is enough of everything to go around. In fact, abundance is all there really is. If abundant good health, wealth or happiness is what you need, align yourself with the natural forces available to you, which include tapping into your inner resources, skills and techniques. You are a natural creator. Your powerhouse is within you and is accessible at all times. A way will be made clear.

Ask yourself what needs are not being met in your life right now. Is now good enough for you? If you are not satisfied with your life as it is now, ask yourself what would make it better and remember you deserve the best. So, don't deny yourself. When the answers do come, you will be in a position to work on attracting them into your life.

There is real power in going with the flow. You cannot oppose the forces at work in your life as this creates resistance and blocks progress. But you can influence the direction things take. Bend. Go around. But stay the course that you have chosen whenever possible and when it is not possible, reexamine and adjust wherever necessary. It may have been that what you wanted was not in your best interest or that there is something else infinitely better than what you previously imagined. It is only in hindsight that you will know for sure.

Learn to say no

This seems such a simple thing to do, but for many it is extremely difficult. We were raised in a society where we were to do as we were told, or felt the need to please others. In order to be true to yourself, however, there will be times when you will need to say no to a request. If you want to work on this there are techniques you can use. One really helpful technique is to practice, when you are alone, possibly before a mirror, saying no in different ways until you become comfortable with it. When an occasion arises you will be better prepared.

Keep an open mind

When overwhelming, angry, sad, nervous or neurotic feelings do come up, don't say or do anything you might regret later. Distance yourself. Take some time to breathe slowly and completely. Exhale all of the air in your lungs before taking in a full breath. By taking a step back and breathing, you will soon begin to feel calmer. Cortisol levels will drop and that fight or flight response will be stilled enough for you to begin to think more clearly and to act more appropriately going forward. Let overwhelming things sit for just a little while as they may appear differently with other facts taken into consideration.

Next, send love into the situation, thereby dispelling fear and anxiety to clear a way forward that is more productive. Call forth clarity, peace of mind and assistance in dealing with these issues. This will reign in impulsive reactions to situations and circumstances.

Too often we are only able to see **"all or nothing"** solutions to problems. More often than not there are soulful solutions that can be seen as a middle ground, allowing for a **"this and"** possibility. There will be creative solutions available to meet your needs.

This is not to say that you are to ignore your gut feelings, but when you are afraid, angry, sad, unsure, exhausted or overwhelmed, just know and remember that everything is going to be alright. **It will be OK.**

Only make life-altering decisions when you are feeling safe, calm, efficient, clear headed. You don't want your emotions dictating the results entirely. They are a consideration to be sure, but would you make the same decisions when you are feeling less triggered? Remember to consider what is in your best interest and act on that.

Originality

Don't compare yourself to anyone, as you may feel that you will never quite measure up. Nobody is watching. No one really knows or cares, so just be yourself.

You are unique and should be aiming for originality in what you think, say and do. Only you can create a better life for yourself, but you are not without assistance and guidance along the way.

By expanding your consciousness and working in the positive, using your gifts, abilities, skills and techniques to illuminate and forge the path towards what you have consciously and sub-consciously sown, you will get there.

Potential

Your unique path will lead you to realizing your untapped potential. Your purpose now should be in discovering and actualizing the potential that is uniquely yours. Yet, somehow we fill our days and find little to no time has been dedicated to our personal development. Our untapped potential remains on the sidelines of life. The moment we are bored we fill it with diversions.

It is in the stillness that we create. We need to find some time for ourselves to just be in the stillness, to connect with ourselves and to listen to our heart's desires. After all, we are creating our own reality so we can factor in the time to connect, to heal, to grow, and to create in the positive.

What gets in the way of being able to realize your potential? Often it is an entrenched false presupposition that you never questioned. Challenge these in the light of day. Begin there and make self-emancipation your new priority, your new project. Your path will be laid bare.

False presuppositions

False presuppositions or negative beliefs that you hold about yourself are often baseless and incorrect. They are instrumental in keeping your stuck. You internalized them from your cultural milieu without ever questioning them. You just lived as if they were true and made decisions from there: Beliefs like: **"I'm not _____ enough." "I'd love to ____ but ___." "You can't make any money in ____." "Forget it, you'll never be able to ____." Fill in the blanks.** Just to name a few.

Debunk, flip or cancel those beliefs as they hinder your development and sabotage your progress.

Perspective

Look at recurring issues from different perspectives. Allow your mind to view things from a completely different angle. There are as many solutions as there are perspectives. Pick what works for you.

Positive self-talk

Our inner voices have a lot of power over how we perceive ourselves to be. Listen to your inner voices and replace all critical, negative, stultifying self-talk with positive, life affirming self-talk and work from there. Over time this will become habitual. You are still dealing with the issues at hand. You are not glossing over them, but you are choosing your thoughts more wisely. Silence and flip those negative voices into positive ones and observe the results over time. This will open you up to new possibilities, putting you onto a new path, to think, act and receive in the positive.

Perseverance and persistence is the key. Positivity is a state of mind.

Quests and Questions

As someone in search of a more fulfilling, happier life, you are a seeker on the path of self-emancipation. No small task. The important words here are quest and questions.

If you are not aware of what you want in your life, you will need to ask yourself relevant and pertinent questions. Pay attention to what arises as this will focus your quest.

Have an honest talk with yourself. Formulate questions that will bring you more clarity. Dig down to the level of what is missing in your life and what its opposite attributes would include. When the answers do come they will ring true and give you something to aim at attracting into your life.

Ask, seek and knock with this in mind. Once you have done this with sincerity, passion and compassion, make your demands and leave your demands to be answered in their own time. Remember, faith over time creates.

Pay attention to the cues

Opportunities, information and help will come in many unusual or unexpected ways. Pay attention to the cues that are provided. All you need to do is your part by being discerning based on whether you are receiving a gift, a lesson, or a test. This can be tricky but with time you will know the difference; in either case, it won't matter. You have your lifetime to devote to your quest. There is no time frame.

Reality

Your reality is not the same as anyone's in the world. We make it up as we go along. So, how do you see your reality? What would you like to change? What do you need help with? Repetitively living your life unsatisfactorily is no longer necessary when you realize that your reality is completely up to you. What do you think, feel, want and need?

Realize how you got where you are now and aim for where you want to be by tweaking or changing the route you previously took. If you don't know how, just go within and set the course for assistance and guidance for the highest good into action.

Rewrite the script

A certain script has been written up to now, but if you are not satisfied with it, rewrite it. Bit by bit. Only you have that ability.

Don't like a habitual pattern of yours? Replace it with one that you do like. Do it your way. Replace the old with the new.

Routines

Routines can be put in place that will replace old habits. Instead of fighting the demons of negativity in your life, flip them into their positive opposites and head in that direction with what you ask, seek, think, say and do.

Responsibility

Your development is your personal responsibility. It is your primary responsibility. Everything else is just secondary. No one else can do it for you, although many people may help or hinder your progress along the way. Ultimately, you are the only one responsible for your life.

Results come over time

Just as your existence is the result of your prior thoughts, actions and experiences over time, you most definitely will see positive results in due time when working more consciously in the positive, as like attracts like. Positivity begets more to be positive for.

Inner Sanctum

Always remember that you have within you a sacred place where you can go to find peace, safety, wisdom and assistance with whatever it is that you are at work with. There is no limit to access. It's always available to you. No matter what your circumstances may be.

Stuck

If you find that you are slipping back into old habits just notice this and turn things around by acting on new opportunities to use your skills and techniques like meditating, I-Watching-Me and championing yourself with positive self-talk, honesty, sincerity, compassion, integrity, taking stock and going within. This will get you back on track. Do this whenever you feel stuck. Be your own best friend.

Simplify

Simplify things down to their causes and effects: **if this, then that...** All is cause and effect. Therefore, if you want to change the effects on your life you must look at changing the real true causes. Start working from here. Ask your pertinent questions. Do your seeding, asking, seeking and knocking. Learn and look for answers as to why you are stuck or why you don't feel content or safe.

Safe

By becoming aware that you are much more than the sum of your parts, you will begin to feel safer, guided, guarded and protected in your process of sowing the seeds of change in your life. You are not without assistance going forward. Go about creating your life's garden by doing what needs to be done. It is a unique experience, but you are living with all you need. You are perfect, whole and complete, perfect in your imperfections.

Don't sabotage your potential, joy, gifts, desires, dreams or interests.

Sabotage

Saboteurs like apathy, procrastination, low self-esteem, insecurity, powerlessness, ignorance, lethargy, fear, shame, guilt, poverty, or simply being too busy are all stultifying. Weed these out and replace them with their opposites. Rise above the negative saboteurs. They aren't real.

Story

Everyone has their "story". The story, although valid, is what we tell ourselves and others about our pasts. But that is all the story is: the past. If we stay stuck in the past, we sabotage our chances of making real life changes. As an adult you are the author of your own story now.

Stretch

Stretch both your mind and your body to eliminate the rigidity that can set in. Move: gardening, yoga, tai chi, martial arts, music, dance, sport, biking, swimming, walking, etc. You don't need to take the course or buy the shoes. Just do what comes naturally and go with the flow. The discipline and focus will do you some good. Be invested in your physical and mental health and allow yourself to have fun on a regular basis. After a while, if you stick with it, you'll look forward to the activity and wonder what you would ever do without it in your life.

If a shortage of money or time are issues, then simply do whatever you enjoy doing right there at home. Find a spot you are comfortable in and move, sing, dance, play, etc.

Switch it up

If we only investigate one track of our interests in life we will have missed out on maximizing our potential. There is an infinite number of things you can try. And even if you can't try it all, you will have allowed yourself a broader scope and potential for fun.

So many people are of the belief that since they can no longer do whatever it was that gave them joy, due to illness, age or physical limitations, they close the door to other challenging opportunities for joy and are miserably bored, frustrated and disconnected from what gives them joy.

Look around you. Search out what is available that is of interest to you. Often there are opportunities right beneath our noses, but we never considered them for ourselves. Perhaps we can.

Thoughts

Thoughts are energy and energy is matter, so, watch your thoughts. They matter more than you may realize. They are the grid-work of your emotions. First there is a thought, or deep-seated belief, then there is an emotion. They are your powerhouse, your inert resource. So choose them wisely, lovingly and compassionately, but above all truthfully.

Watch your thoughts from a loving but discerning place. See the patterns that emerge between thoughts and feelings. Ask yourself how your thoughts make you feel. Are they helping or hindering you?

No one can tell you what to think, how to think or when to think. You are the master here. Sometimes thoughts have a tendency to run away with us, but we have the power to reign them back in.

When you look in on your thoughts and find that your mind is engaging in self pity, cynicism, sarcasm, negativity, anger, spiteful inner dialogues with imaginary people, take some time to send love into the situation. Perhaps it would be good to understand why you are being triggered, instead of harboring angry thoughts which only serves to validate your dissatisfaction with a sense of being right, but you remain stuck with the negativity. By sending love into the situation you dispel the negativity. You give it up to be resolved for the highest good and let it go. Pick your battles wisely. Things will turn around quickly and creative solutions to the problems will be made clear.

Catch yourself in the act of destructive thinking and take control of your thoughts. Look at things with a rational and calm mind when the storm blows over. If you only let anger and disappointment cloud your judgment, well then when you no longer feel angry or disappointed, your impetus will be gone for rational or creative change and things will remain as they were until the next time. Sometimes that is just fine because the problems were insignificant in the broader scheme of things, while at other times, it is a cog in the wheel of positive change and creativity when you know something has to be done and no longer have the impetus to carry it out to your own detriment or the detriment of others.

If you find yourself being triggered into senselessly going around in a negative downward spiral of thought, simply notice this and say: "**Cancel. Cancel.**" Your thoughts will be redirected. You will have taken back the moment and taken control of your thoughts.

When rational thought is given to the situation, the truth of what you should or should not do will eventually be clear. Only you have the ability to stop things from being blown out of proportion or from causing a train wreck in your life by being aware of the way you think.

Thoughts and therefore emotions come and go. If you find your thoughts and emotions are in a jumbled mess, don't make any rash decisions that you may regret later when those thoughts are gone. Wait for things to settle down first and then reassess honestly. Is this what you want? Is this in any way destructive to you? What should you do about it? Do you need help? Look for unchecked assumptions.

When you find that your peaceful flow of thoughts has been disrupted with constant nagging ones, take some time to yourself, close your eyes, slowly blow or exhale all of the air from your lungs before breathing in a full relaxing breath and go within for the help you need in getting through this. Connect to your personal power and stay in your truth.

Transformation

Ultimately, transformation on any level requires that you trust over time and stay in your truth.

Trust

First, you must trust in the process that is you. You are an enigma unto yourself. Trust yourself — body, soul and Spirit. Take some time to get grounded in the moment and to develop trust in yourself, your whole Self.

Time

It might take time to develop an intimate relationship with all the levels of yourself, but half an hour a day is not much to ask for you to connect and begin the process of working with all of the odds in your favour.

Unhappy

By giving yourself unconditional love and unconditional forgiveness, you unlock and unearth potential for good to come into your life. You must not underestimate or undervalue the power of love to transform any situation you find yourself in that has you feeling uncomfortable or unhappy — since those negative feelings are fear-based and love has the power to transmute and transform them.

Understand that whenever things are unclear and there is trepidation around the unknown, you have unlimited strength in the resources available to you when you unite your body, soul and Spirit and put the problems forward for clarification and resolution in a loving and truthful manner.

Eureka!

Truth has a ring to it that you automatically recognize. Those Eureka! moments, those AHA! moments are valuable pieces of the puzzle that you are at work with in life. Pay closer attention to them. Sometimes they are answers to heartfelt questions or validations and recognition that you are on the right track.

Validation

We all need to be validated and accepted for the special persons that we are. By virtue of the fact that you are alive, you are a valuable, viable human being. Never doubt or undervalue yourself or your potential for good.

The famous humanitarian, philosopher and theologian, Albert Schweitzer's principle is: **I am life that wills to live in the midst of other life that wills to live.**

Perhaps it really is as simple as this. We must value ourselves and others, but what other people think, say or do should not affect how we feel about our own value. We must not allow ourselves to be enmeshed with others' expectations of us to our detriment and become victims of circumstance, feeling powerless to effect positive change.

We need to validate and champion ourselves. We need to be our own best friend.

Vulnerability

Feelings of vulnerability frighten many of us away from actively taking charge of our lives and venturing forth into the unknown. But, if all can be reduced to mutable laws then we are vibrational frequencies, and if we don't like the vibes in and around us, then we have the power and the responsibility to change them regardless of the fears they engender.

Change begins within first. Others may genuinely love and respect you and will support your growth. There may be others with a hidden agenda who feel they have something to lose if you change. They might try to dissuade you, but don't let them stop you. If necessary, when dealing with negative or controlling people in your life, keep things to yourself and forge ahead.

Vision

Focus your vision on the abundance and beauty that exists for you to claim in your life. Set your sights high and accept that or better for the highest good of all concerned.

Worry

Eliminate worry by using your gifts, new-found skills, techniques and tools and know that you are not alone. Worrying is just another fear-based, noxious weed stemming from fear-based thoughts like: **what if...** It doesn't serve anyone. You can work from within to let this go by giving it up to your High Self to work on and by sowing those seeds of loving and rational thought to dispel the fears that overwhelm you.

Wisdom

Connect to and heed your wisdom by listening to that peaceful, loving voice that wants only the best for you.

Wisdom can come from within but it can also come to you via a friend or loved one, something someone said, a book that you might come across, or a dream. Those nuggets of wisdom are to be acknowledged, cherished and acted upon if they are sound and are clear answers to your heartfelt questions. They are not to be ignored.

Wonder

Dare to wonder — whether you know it or not, you are truly wonderful!

Self-worth

What do you want? Whatever it takes, you are worth it!

Write your own script

Expectations

What are your expectations? Do they inspire you, cause anxiety or cynicism based on previous disappointments and pain? Revamp them.

You can write, draw, paint, collage, sculpt, whittle or construct an image of your expectations. Keep it in plain view so that you can look at it regularly in order to stay on track. This will focus your attention and remind you of your desires.

Exceptions

There are rules and exceptions to those rules, but your uniqueness is exceptional. You are exceptional — no exception.

Exercise

The most important exercise you will ever have to do is to exercise your right to choose and then to apply the laws of the universe to attract or attain your desired outcomes. Use the tools available to you. Go within. Sow those seeds of positivity and creative change. Champion and communicate with your pure Self or the Powers that Be and keep the faith. Experience fully the life you are creating as it is filled with innumerable lessons and gifts.

It's OK to be you

You have a contribution to make by being the very one you came here to be. No one else on the planet is like you. You are special. Whatever it is you have done, are doing, or will do in the future matters.

While you live, you are ultimately only accountable to yourself. The two questions you may ask yourself, that you will be accountable for when you leave this world are: **"How have I loved?" and "What have I done with my gifts?"**

Zeal

Aiming for and working towards positive change renews within us a zeal for life. It gives us a focus, direction and hope. We can have a restored sense of personal power zapping through us.

Hold onto this power. If it slips away, reclaim it. It is always there for you to tap into. All you need to do is to have that championing talk with yourself; sit quietly and go within to connect to your High Self. Breathe. Relax. State your emotionalized commands in the positive. Let go and move forward from here with gratitude. Do this as often as you need to. Unconditionally.

Be aware of what comes to you over time — of the challenges, changes, opportunities, ideas, people, situations. Pay attention. A way forward will be made clear. There will be lessons, sign posts, twists and turns, hills and valleys on your garden path — all leading you to reaping the harvest you have sown.

Whenever you find you are struggling to create or doubt your attempts, remember that in nature there are times when the seeds you have sown only seem to lie fallow. Remember that your etheric blueprint is lovingly, carefully being germinated, fertilized and cared for behind the scenes. The ground work has been laid. The process is in motion.

Enjoy the garden of your life. As in all gardens, there are times of seeding, nourishing, caring for and cultivating, as well as reaping the abundance of what you have sown.

Enjoy nourishing your life with the cornucopia of your creation and share it with those that you love.